BEOWULF

THE WARRIOR

retold by
IAN SERRAILLIER

illustrated
by
SEVERIN

BETHLEHEM BOOKS • IGNATIUS PRESS
BATHGATE, N.D.   SAN FRANCISCO

Text © 1954 Anne Serraillier
Illustrations © Oxford University Press (1954)
Reprinted from *Beowulf the Warrior by Serraillier*
(1954) by permission of Oxford
University Press.

Introduction and special features
© 1994 by Bethlehem Books

First Bethlehem Books printing, June 1994

ISBN 978-1-883937-03-4

Library of Congress catalog number: 94–70289

Cover art by Severin
Cover design by Davin Carlson

Bethlehem Books • Ignatius Press
10194 Garfield Street South
Bathgate, ND 58216
www.bethlehembooks.com

Printed in the United States on acid free paper

BEOWULF

THE WARRIOR

C O N T E N T S

INTRODUCTION

This retelling of *Beowulf* has been enjoyed by a wide range of ages ever since it first came out in 1954. Ian Serraillier has worked from the original text, staying true to the story and the poetic description of the Old English poem, but recasting them in a blank verse narrative style, much more accessible to modern ears. It reads aloud wonderfully well, meeting different readers or listeners at their varying levels of understanding. We know a four-year-old entranced by its rhythms and earthy vocabulary; an eleven-year-old fascinated by the heroic adventures; older ones intrigued by the setting; and all ages moved by Beowulf's brave, sad ending. There is a primordial appeal in the epic's story of monster-slaying; but in its verse is the attraction of a tale both vigorously and hauntingly told. There could be no better introduction than this one to the classic *Beowulf*.

Beowulf is the earliest of all extant epics composed in a northern European language. Most scholars date it to the 8th century. Not only is *Beowulf* an early epic; it is a very thoughtfully composed one. It also deserves our attention as a work permeated with the Christian consciousness of a recently converted Anglo-Saxon people. These characteristics are faithfully transmitted in this version.

The subject matter of *Beowulf* is Scandinavian and Germanic, not Anglo-Saxon. The story and setting are drawn from Denmark and Geatland in 6th century heathen times. This is, after all, the region from whence the Saxons came to England. But the treatment of that material reveals a Christian mind ennobling the character of Beowulf and envisioning his battles in a wider moral context. Beowulf's victories are more than just supernaturally prodigious. Beowulf's enemies, Grendel and his hag mother, descend from the world's first murderer, Cain; the monstrous dragon likewise is readily aligned with all that is evil and that resists the forces of right. Beowulf, ultimately giving his life for his people, destroys these powers. We grieve at his death because, "of all the kings of the world," he is "mightiest in valor, in his ways, the mildest, most kind to his people and keenest for praise." He meets his death as fate wills and also, we are made to feel, in the presence of an Almighty God controlling even fate.

When one realizes that *Beowulf* had been completely lost to English society for centuries and was returned to our consciousness through the discovery of a single manuscript dating to the 900's—itself singed and barely surviving a library fire—one begins to prize the old, old voice with its rare message from a living past. Since the first printing of the text, in 1815, the epic has been much studied.

We think readers will find the story, atmosphere, and themes of *Beowulf* conveyed here again with strength and eloquence. "Readers," we say. But remember, listeners and reciters of the text are to be encouraged—reciters of all ages and skill; included are those who read aloud. The poetry of this retelling beckons an oral recitation, as of old, when minstrels handed on the tale. With this shorter version ringing in their ears, older youth and adults will more readily move on to full-length renditions of this classic epic. Meanwhile, let the little ones come; they will absorb the language and spirit of *Beowulf* and perhaps surprise you with their own oral transmission of the tale:

"Over the misty moor came Grendel . . . ."

Lydia Reynolds
Bethlehem Books
Spring, 1994

TO
GERALD AND
ROSALIND

GRENDEL

HROTHGAR, King of the Danes, glorious in
battle,
Built him a huge hall—its gleaming roof
Towering high to heaven—strong to withstand
The buffet of war. He called it Heorot
And lived there with his Queen. At time of feasting
He gave to his followers rings and ornaments
And bracelets of bright gold, cunningly wrought,
Graved with runes and deeds of dead heroes.
Here they enjoyed feasts and high fellowship,
Story and song and the pride of armed peace.
But away in the treacherous fens, beyond the moor,
A hideous monster lurked, fiend from hell,
Misbegotten son of a foul mother,
Grendel his name, hating the sound of the harp,
The minstrel's song, the bold merriment of men
In whose distorted likeness he was shaped
Twice six feet tall, with arms of hairy gorilla
And red ferocious eyes and ravening jaws.
He, one night, when the warriors of Hrothgar lay
Slumbering after banquet, came to Heorot,
Broke down the door, seized in his fell grip
A score and more of the sleeping sons of men
And carried them home for meat. At break of day
The hall of Heorot rang loud and long
With woe of warriors and grief of the great King.
Thereafter, from dark lake and dripping caves
Night after night over the misty moor
Came Grendel, gross and grim, famished for flesh.
Empty the beds, no man dared sleep at Heorot,
But Grendel smelt them out of their hiding place,
And many a meal he made of warriors.
For twelve years he waged war with Hrothgar,
Piling grief upon grief. For twelve years
He haunted great Heorot.

Now there lived overseas
In the land of the Geats a youth of valiance abounding,
Mightiest yet mildest of men, his name Beowulf,
Who, hearing of Grendel and minded to destroy him,
Built a boat of the stoutest timber and chose him
Warriors, fourteen of the best. In shining armour
They boarded the great vessel, beached on the shingle
By the curling tide. Straightway they shoved her off.
They ran up the white sail. And the wind caught her,
The biting wind whipped her over the waves.
Like a strong bird the swan-boat winged her way
Over the grey Baltic, the wintry whale-road,
Till the lookout sighted land—a sickle of fair sand,
And glittering white cliffs. The keel struck
The shingle. The warriors sprang ashore.

4

But the watchman of the Danes, the lone cliff guardian,
Seeing them from afar, spurred his charger and came
Galloping down to the shore. He brandished his spear
And over the wind and wave-roar loud he shouted:
'Strangers from the whale-road, who are you that dare,
Unbidden, unheralded, so boldly trespass here ?
Upon your flashing shields and the points of your spears
I see the glint of death.'

And Beowulf answered:
'We are from Sweden, O guardian of the shore. Fear not,
For in loyalty we come—from friendly fields
That tremble to the tale of your suffering and horror
Unspeakable. Crowding sail, hot haste we are come
With stout spears of ashwood and shields to protect you.

God grant we rid you of Grendel the grim monster!'
  The watchman lowered his spear, and from smiling lips
The wind blew to Beowulf fair words of greeting:
'Whoever serves my King is welcome here.
Come, noble warriors, let me show you the way,
And my men will look to your boat.'

                They left her at anchor,
The broad-bellied ship afloat on the bobbing tide,
And followed him over the cliff toward Heorot. As they
      marched,
The boar-head glared from their helmets, the iron rings
Rang on their mailcoats. And the watchman said, 'Behold
The huge hall, wide-gabled, the gleaming roof
Towering high to heaven. Follow the street

To the studded door, where Wulfgar, herald of the King,
Will receive you. May God Almighty prosper your
    venture
And hold you safe!' He wheeled about on his horse
And galloped away to the shore.

                        Thus came the warriors
To Heorot and, heavy with weariness, halted by the door.
They propped their spears by a pillar; from blistered
    hands
Their shields slid clattering to the floor. Then Wulfgar,
Herald of the King, having demanded their errand,
Ran to his royal master and quick returning
Urged them within. The long hall lay before them,
The floor paved with stone, the roof high-raftered.
In mournful state upon his throne sat brooding
Aged Hrothgar, grey-haired and bowed with grief.
Slowly he raised his eyes, leaden, lustreless,
And gazed upon the youth as with ringing step
Boldly he strode forth till he stood at his feet.
    'O noble Hrothgar, giver of treasure,
Lord of the rousing war-song, we bring you greeting.
Because we grieve deep for your desolation,
Over the long paths of the ocean have we laboured,
I and my warriors, to rid you of the brute
That nightly robs you of rest. I am no weakling.
With my trusty blade I have slain a monster brood
And blindly at night many a foul sea-beast
That writhed and twisted in the bounding wave.
I beg you to grant my wish. I shall not fail.'
    Then Hrothgar stretched out his arms in welcome
And took him by the hand and said, 'Beowulf,
I knew you as a child, and who has not exulted
In your fame as a fighter? It is a triumph song
That ocean thunders to her farthest shore,
It is a whisper in the frailest sea-shell.

Now, like your princely father long ago,
In the brimming kindness of your heart you have come
To deliver us.'

But Unferth bristled at these
words—
Unferth, who sat always at the feet of Hrothgar,
A grovelling, jealous man who could not bear
That anyone should win more fame than he.
   'Braggart!' he cried. 'Are you not that Beowulf
Who failed against Breca in the swimming match?
Seven nights you wallowed in the wintry sea—
Some sport that was!—sport for jeering waves
That jollied you like spindrift from crest to crest
Till, sick with cold, you shrieked for mercy. Who
      heard?
Not Breca, who long since had battled to land,
But the sea, tired at last of its puny plaything,
Spewed you ashore.'

Angrily Beowulf answered:
'That's a drunkard's tale! True, Breca was first
Ashore, but I could have raced him had I wished.
We were boys then, with our full share of folly,
Plunging—sword in hand—giddily to battle
With monster whales, when a storm came sweeping
      down
And gruesome waves ground and trampled us under.
It was Breca that cried for help—I fought to save him,
But a fierce north-easter whipped us apart
And I saw him no more. In the dark and bitter cold,
The icy brine was heaving murkily with monsters.
Glad was I of my sword and mail-coat—for a serpent
Had wound his sinewy coils about my waist,
And squeezing, dragged me below. But before he could
      break me,

9

I slew him—nine others too before the raging floodtide
Rolled me to land. . . .
I am not aware that you, brave Unferth, can boast
Such a record. If you be as bold as you proclaim,
Tell me, how comes it that Grendel is still alive?
Ha, I know a coward when I see one! Soon,
If the King be willing, I shall grapple with Grendel
And show you what courage means.'

                    Then Hrothgar, marking
The warrior's blazing eyes, and hasty hand
Fingering his sword-hilt, with mild words melted his
      anger.
'Noble Beowulf, pay no heed to Unferth,
An envious, wayward man, unworthy of note.
Right gladly I grant your wishes—but first, one word
Of warning. That sword you spoke of—it will avail
Nothing with Grendel, whose life is proof against
All weapons whatsoever, wrought by man.
You must go for him with your hands, your bare
      hands.'

Thus spake King Hrothgar and from his bounteous
      heart
Wished the youth well. Soon as the benches
Had been cleared away for banquet, he called for his
      Queen,
The gracious Wealhtheow who, proudly entering,
Was proudly hailed by royal clarion of trumpets.
A gown of broidered gold she wore, behind her
A long train, dark as the night sky,
Illumined with galaxy of stars that, as she glided
Forward to greet her guests, trembled in the torchlight.
The mead cup glowed in her hands, strong to revive
      them
Weary from wandering over the surging sea.

Kneeling, she offered it first to Beowulf, next
To his warriors each in turn, and lastly to the Danes.
They drank and they feasted, the jewelled goblets
        clashed
In the great hall. There was loud revelry of heroes,
Bold merriment of men, and minstrel song
And the soothing voice of the harp—until twilight,
The drowsy hour of Grendel's coming, the black shape
Stealing over the dusky moor. Then the Danes
Man by man uprose and, clearing the banquet,
Brought for their guests soft couches, pillow-strewn,
With fleeces of thick wool. When the Queen had
        departed,
They hurried each to his secret hiding place;
And last of all, murmuring abundant blessing
On Beowulf—grave and reluctant, the noble Hrothgar.

  Straightway Beowulf stripped off his armour, his
        mailcoat,
His shining helmet. His shield and precious sword
Gave he to his servant, and in the ring of warriors
Lay down to rest. But spent as they were—
For tumult of Grendel and his havoc, like runaway
        hooves
Making riot in their brains—they could not sleep.
Under their fleeces in terror they sweated and trembled,
Wide-awake, till at last, outworn with weariness,
Heavy-lidded, they slept—all but Beowulf.
Alone, he watched.

                    Over the misty moor
From the dark and dripping caves of his grim lair,
Grendel with fierce ravenous stride came stepping.
A shadow under the pale moon he moved,
That fiend from hell, foul enemy of God,
Toward Heorot. He beheld it from afar, the gleaming roof

Towering high to heaven. His tremendous hands
Struck the studded door, wrenched it from the hinges
Till the wood splintered and the bolts burst apart.
Angrily he prowled over the polished floor,
A terrible light in his eyes—a torch flaming!
As he scanned the warriors, deep-drugged in sleep,
Loud loud he laughed, and pouncing on the nearest
Tore him limb from limb and swallowed him whole,
Sucking the blood in streams, crunching the bones.
Half-gorged, his gross appetite still unslaked,
Greedily he reached his hand for the next—little
      reckoning
For Beowulf. The youth clutched it and firmly grappled.

Such torture as this the fiend had never known.
In mortal fear, he was minded to flee to his lair,
But Beowulf prisoned him fast. Spilling the benches,
They tugged and heaved, from wall to wall they hurtled.
And the roof rang to their shouting, the huge hall
Rocked, the strong foundations groaned and trembled.
Then Grendel wailed from his wound, his shriek of
      pain
Roused the Danes in their hiding and shivered to the
      stars.
The warriors in the hall spun reeling from their couches,
In dull stupor they fumbled for their swords, forgetting
No man-made weapon might avail. Alone, Beowulf
Tore Grendel's arm from his shoulder asunder,
Wrenched it from the root while the tough sinews
      cracked.
And the monster roared in anguish, well knowing
That deadly was the wound and his mortal days ended.
Wildly lamenting, away into the darkness he limped,
Over the misty moor to his gloomy home.
But the hero rejoiced in his triumph and wildly waved
In the air his blood-soaked trophy.

And the sun,
God's beacon of brightness, banishing night,
Made glad the sky of morning. From near and far
The Danes came flocking to Heorot to behold
The grisly trophy—Grendel's giant arm
Nailed to the wall, the fingertips outspread,
With nails of sharpened steel and murderous spikes
Clawing the roof. Having drunk their fill of wonder,
Eagerly they followed his track to the lake, and there
Spellbound they stared at the water welling with blood,
Still smoking hot where down to the joyless deep
He had dived, downward to death. And they praised
    Beowulf
And swore that of all men under the sun, beyond
    measure
Mightiest was he and fittest to govern his people.

   Meanwhile, in the hall at Heorot the grateful King,
All glooming gone, his countenance clear and cloudless
As the sky in open radiance of the climbing sun,
Gave thanks to God for deliverance. 'Beowulf,' he said,
'Bravest of men, I shall love you now as my son.
All I have is yours for the asking. Take
What treasure you will. But first let us feast and be
    merry.'

   Straightway they washed the blood from the floor,
    propped up
The battered door; the drooping walls they draped
With embroidery, bright hangings of woven gold.
There was drinking and feasting again, revelry of heroes,
And the jewelled goblets clashed. At last the King,
Aged Hrothgar, grey-haired giver of treasure,
Ordered gifts to be brought. To Beowulf he gave
A sword and mailcoat and banner of gleaming gold;
A plated helmet so tough no steel might cleave it;

Eight prancing horses with golden harness
And bridles of silver, the proudest saddled with his own
Battle-seat, all set with splendid jewels,
Most cunningly inlaid; to each of the warriors
A sword and bountiful recompense of gold
For their friend that Grendel slew.

                     Then the minstrel sang
Of rousing deeds of old. Like flames in the firelight
The heart leapt to hear them. And when he had done
And the harp lay silent, the Queen of the Danes spoke
      out:
'Beowulf, dearest youth, son of most favoured
And fortunate of mothers, this your deed is matchless.
Greater than all these. In the farthest corners
of the earth your name shall be known. Wherever the
      ocean
Laps the windy shore and the wave-worn headland,
Your praise shall be sung.'

                     And now the feast was ended.
With final clarion of trumpets they left the hall,
Hrothgar and his gracious Queen, leading Beowulf
To a stately chamber to rest. But the Danes remained
Clearing the banquet. They brought couches spread
With pillows and warm coverlets, and lay down,
Each with his broad shield at his head, his mailcoat,
His spear and shining helmet—as was the custom
Long ere Grendel came. Now fearless of monster,
Their minds were at ease, quiet as the summer sea,
The sparkling water, unmurmuring and serene
Under the moon. In comfort of spirit, in blessed
Trust and tranquillity they sank to rest.

GRENDEL'S MOTHER

OVER the misty moor, under the dark
vault of heaven a shadow came gliding—
a she-monster,
Mother of Grendel. From the chill waters of the fenland,
Brooding on her grief, greedy for revenge,
To Heorot she came and broke down the door
And mightily burst the bars asunder. The Danes
In the darkness felt for their spears—with drowsy
fumbling,
Their slow arms shackled heavily with sleep.
A stride she measured over the polished floor
To the wall, where Grendel's grisly arm was fixed,
The fingertips outspread, spattered with blood.
Fiercely she tore it from the nail and, snatching
A warrior from his couch, in surly triumph
Shouldered him and swiftly, with double spoil,

Sneaked over the hills to her lair. . . But Beowulf,
Battle-weary, was sleeping in his chamber—of this
    tumult
Heard he nothing.

        At sunrise he marched with his comrades
To Hrothgar, to bring him morning greeting in the hall,
But the grey-haired giver of treasure answered him sadly:
'Ask not for happiness, for grief is heaven's decree
And there is no singing in the morning stars.
Brave Aeschere is dead, my counsellor and friend,
By Grendel's mother—as he slept—most foully,
Most treacherously slain. She made off with him
Over the moor to her den—to the lonely land
Where dwell the dark spirits, by paths of peril,
By cloud-haunted hills where wolves go hunting,
By windy cliffs where swollen torrents tumbling
Plunge headlong into the misty deep,
The grumbling under-water. A mile beyond
There lies an evil lake no plummet has sounded,
The margin all along with the roots entangled
Of tall trees; in gloomy splendour they rise,
Their branches feathered with frost. Yonder at night
A horror can be seen—the cold flood on fire,
With candles kindling the dark till quenched at dawning
To a grey smoulder. Of that dread water
No beast dare drink. The proud-antlered deer—
Hard-pressed in the chase, with clamourous hounds at
    heel—
Would sooner die than touch it. O weird and evil
Is the Grendel lake! When stormy wind is stirring,
The angry wave leaps up to lash the cloud
And the air darkens and the bloated heavens weep. . .
O Beowulf, dear as a son to me, you alone
Can deliver us—if you will.'
                    He ended, and Beowulf

20

Proud youth of valiance abounding, spoke out:
'I am not afraid, O King. I snap my fingers
In the face of death, for fame is worth the seeking.'
Then, Hrothgar in gladness grasped him by the shoulder
And for his daring offered him bountiful reward—
Rings and bright armour and treasure manifold.
But noble Beowulf, heedless of gain, hastily
Brushed the words aside and bade him be patient
And to the place of horror lead him straightway.

The King saddled his war-steed, proud champion
Of the curling mane, and then, summoning his guard,
Led them from Heorot. Beside him in shining armour
Strode Beowulf and his warriors. And the wild moor
Was stunned with their tramping, the hills and the wolf
        crags
Rang as they marched with the clink of mailed men.
By paths of peril he led them, to the lonely land
Where the dark spirits dwell, by the cloven mountain
And the cataract madly careering, by the torrent tumbling
In plunge perpetual over the dizzy brink
To the darkness below. And at last they came to the lake
All lined with trees, with their plumage of frost and
        tangled
Trailing roots. There, fixed on the cliff, they beheld
A grisly sight—the head of noble Aeschere,
Their counsellor and friend, his white face channelled
With tracery of red, his hair clotted and damp,
Mist-cold—and below, at their feet the dark water,
Foaming and gurgling, bubbling hot with blood.
At once Beowulf unslung his battle-horn
And pressed it to his lips. The long shrill note
Cut the clean wind; the cold cliff,
Echoing, replied. Whereat a weird head
Rose dripping from the lake and gazed upon Beowulf
With stony wondering eyes; then another,

Thick-crusted, bristling with scales, his tusks
All hung with weed; and dragons too, bold
Sea-devils, all manner of evil monster,
Till all the lake was a-gleam with eyes, luminous,
Amazed. And now they were moving, long serpents
Looping the sluggish wave, in slow undulation
Heaving huge coils from the murky deep;
And one, bolder than his fellows, came speeding toward
     them,
Slithering over the foam. The King marked him
And, swiftly fitting an arrow, let fly and struck
To the heart. What a wailing was there as, thrashing its
     tail,
Mid showering spears it laboured slowly ashore,
Slowly and more slowly. They dragged it dead
From the water, all stuck with steel, to their feet.
And lo, when they looked again, the lake was empty
Of monsters—some the gluttonous pool had swallowed,
While others over the rocks with angry howling

Scrambled to their dens.
                              Then in a loud voice
Beowulf cried, 'Where is Grendel's mother?
Ho there, she-devil, were-wolf of the lake,
Quit your hiding!' He raised his battle-horn
And pressed it to his lips. The long shrill note
Cut the clean wind; the cold cliff,
Echoing, replied. No answer yielded the deep,
But the water trembled and the wave shuddered for fear.
Again he cried, 'Coward, do you shrink from battle?
Must I plunge in the mere and seek you out myself?'

Then they clad him in armour: first, his mailcoat,
Hand-wrought with iron links hundred on hundred,
Strong to guard his body from the monster grip;
Next, his helmet with boar's head glaring,
Plated with bands no blade could bite, sparkling
With jewels to light his watery way. And last,
Finest of all, a Danish sword they gave him,
With hilt of twisted gold, of steel infallible,
Hrunting its name. A moment he stood, pondering
Restless in mind, half given to gloom, then spoke:
'O noble Hrothgar, grey-haired giver of treasure,
I am ready to depart. But whether it be that Hrunting
Shall win me fame or death devour me, I know not,
For secret are the ways of Fate, and her word final.
But should I die—I beg you, look to my men;
Give to Unferth my sword, my treasure to Hygelac
My father. Farewell.'
                              He dived into the surge;
The dark wave swallowed him, downward he sank.
Many a savage monster fastened upon him,
With cruel tusk and talon ripped and slashed
His mailcoat—while Grendel's mother, tyrant queen

Of that dismal realm, laughed in her lurking place
Deep at the bottom of the lake. Minded to slay him,
Suddenly lo! with arm outstretched she launched
Upward, straight for Beowulf, and clutched him in her
    claw
And hugged him to her hairy chest so smothering-close
He could not swing his sword, then downward dragged
    him,
Deep down to her den.
                          When the rushing ceased,
He beheld a paved floor unrolling at his feet.
Under the lake in a lofty hall he stood
Whose roof, buttressed with stout rafters, upheld
The weight of water. No drop from above could reach
    him—
And dreamily, O dreamily in his ear sounded
The far-off oozy murmur of the flood. Before him
Huge flames were leaping, and horrid shadows
Dancing in the firelight, whence issued a shape
More massy than the rest, dark-shouldered,
Towering high, like a mountain hiding the sun.
'Twas the foul she-monster, were-wolf of the deep.

Then drew he his sword, Hrunting, the death-dealer,
Prince of a thousand fights. The edge of steel
Slashed home; with clash upon clash it dinned
Its greedy battle-cry into her skull—yet failed him,
Crumpling like a reed. Fearless, he flung it aside,
And, trusting the strength of his hands, seized her by the
    hair,
Wrestling, swung her heavily this way and that
Buffeting and bruising the walls with her crude bulk,
Then bent her to the ground. In a trice, up she reared

Her shaggy frame and, grappling, squashed him down.
Then, like a dizzy sailor trapped in the shrouds
When sea and heaven swing sickening past
As a sudden wave, topheavy, grinds him down
Into the whirl clinging madly, yet struggling
All the while to fight free—so Beowulf
Under the whelming monster was prisoned fast.
But she, softly keening, brooded upon Grendel
Her son—her only son—whom long ago
By the lapping water tenderly herself had suckled;
Whom as a babe she had fended from brute assault
And loved more than her own life; whom Beowulf
Had slain. Boiling for revenge, she drew her knife—
The broad blade glinting in the firelight, her eyes
Gloating—and struck home.

                        Then surely
Must Beowulf have died, there in the monster's hall,
Under the joyless water. But his mailcoat, looped
And ragged though it was, guarded his life-house,
And God Almighty in His wisdom set him free.
The warrior sprang up. On the wall, gleaming, he spied
A tremendous sword (by giants of olden time
Forged in the furnace of the sun), undimmed in lustre,
So cumbrous-huge only a hero could wield it.
He grabbed the golden hilt and, wheeling mightily,
Smote with all his strength. Splintering her bone-rings,
The blade hacked through her neck and felled her at his
    feet,
Stone-dead.

                    Then great Beowulf rejoiced.
Fierce as the summer sun blazed the steel

In his hand, a beacon of brightness lighting the way.
Triumphant he traversed that dismal underworld
Till suddenly he saw the body of Grendel lying,
The shoulder agape where the arm was wrenched away—
Grim reminder of old griefs. How often
Had Grendel, famished for flesh, stolen upon Heorot,
And, breaking the door, seized in his fell grip
A score and more of the sleeping sons of men
And carried them home for meat! O cruel spoil!
Stung by the memory, he raised the magic sword
And struck off the ghastly head. Then a wonder befell.
So poisonous, so burning hot the blood, the blade
Melted—as frost in the sunlight, or as ice melts
When God the Father unfetters the prisoned flood—
It wasted, it withered, till only the hilt remained.
But the blood cascaded upward, curdling the waters,
And the poisoned wave broke red on the brink, at the feet
Of the weary watchers. Then whitebeards shook their
     heads
And muttered sadly that Beowulf for his daring had died.
And Hrothgar, his mind clouded with a great gloom,
Lamented they had lost one matchless in valour,
Dear to him as a son. Gathering his followers,
From the grim headland slowly he led them home.
Only the comrades of Beowulf lingered on,
Sick at heart, with deep longing and despair
Scanning the troubled water.

           Meanwhile the Prince,
Dragging the monster's head, dived upward.
Behind him a myriad bubbles in sparkling trail
Bejewelled his victorious path and, bursting,
Purged the water of poison. With sturdy stroke
Upward he rose, till his hand broke the surface,

His arm upheaving the huge head. And he swam
Lustily to land. The warriors cried out for joy.
They shouted, they thanked God, they ran to meet him.
They splashed into the water and with impatient hands
Pulled him ashore. Speedily they stripped away
His armour, helmet and mailcoat. Grendel's head
They spiked upon a spear—no light burden
For four stalwart henchmen, staggering, to bear—
Then departed from those waters in such wondrous wise
Cleansed of evil, now silent, without stir
Of brute or tiniest wave, marble-still.
From that lonely land, over the mountain they marched
By cataract madly careering, by paths of peril
Over the desolate hills and the wolf-crags,
Over the wild moor homeward to Heorot. And Hrothgar,
Who in mournful state on his throne sat brooding,
Bowed with grief, his heart bleak as a ruin
Where the wind makes riot while in the wintry wood
The night-owl cries—Hrothgar, roused suddenly
By their shout of triumph, flung wide the studded door
And beheld on the threshold Beowulf holding high
Grendel's ghastly head. The Danes gazed
In horror, the mead-cups fell clattering to the floor,
and boldly through the hall with ringing step
The warrior strode, till he stood at the King's feet.
'Lo, noble Hrothgar, Prince of the Spear-Danes,
Two trophies I bring you for lasting token
Of a glorious deed—this head, and shrunk to a hilt,
The sword that severed it.' With proud gladness
        Hrothgar
Received it, golden remnant of the giant's work.
And he praised Beowulf and thanked God for his
        deliverance,
That the long struggle with the monsters was ended at
        last.
Then there was rich feasting, exchange of treasure,

Loud revelry of heroes; with rousing voice
The minstrel sang the mighty deeds of Beowulf.

And the joyous sun, bright candle of the world,
Soared high to heaven. The meadow by the sea
Rang jubilant with prancing horses, loud
With harness bells as Beowulf marched his warriors
To the shore. And when they beheld beached on the
        shingle
The broad-bellied ship beside the curling tide,
His heart leapt for home. Now was the hour
Of leave-taking. And he spoke: 'Noble Hrothgar,
Of all men most learned in grave courtesy,
Sadly we bid you farewell. If in any way
By deeds of battle I can win greater love,
If over the bounding wave I hear word that neighbours
Oppress you or enemies grind you under heel,
Then with a thousand thanes hot haste will I speed
And a thousand spears and a thousand shields to protect
        you.'
    And Hrothgar answered him: 'O strong in wisdom,
Mightiest yet mildest of men, valiant Beowulf,
Never have I known a youth speak more nobly
Or battle more bravely. You have forged between our
        peoples
So fast a bond that all treason and bloodshed
Of bygone years shall cease. Henceforth our minds,
Not choked with hatred like a thunder sky
But in mutual trust abiding, shall beget peace.
The barren sea between us shall blossom with ships,
With throng of masts—a forest winged with sail—
All laden with treasure (love-token of friends),
And many a man shall greet his fellow with gifts
Over the surging water, the seagulls' way.'
Then Hrothgar, the grey-haired king, giver of treasure,
Embraced him, clinging to his neck and weeping

bitterly
As if his heart would break.

                                When the Danes had shoved her
Clear of the shingle, the warriors leapt aboard.
They ran up the white sail. And the wind caught her,
The biting wind whipped her over the waves.
With timbers groaning, her curved prow scattering the
        foam,
Like a strong bird the swan-boat winged her way
Over the grey Baltic, the wintry whale-road,
Over the long paths of the ocean, on
And ever onward,
Till at last they beheld the shining cliffs of home.
The coastguard, spent with long weary watching,
Hailed them from afar. The keel struck the sand.
Proud, exultant, the warriors leapt to land.

THE FIRE DRAGON

AFTER Hygelac was dead and Heardred had
         been slain,
         Then Beowulf, strong in valour as in wisdom,
Mightiest yet mildest of men, for fifty years
Reigned over his people in peace and prosperity
Unchallenged. From youth of fighting and heroic deeds
Quietly he journeyed toward the tomb, until,
Old at last—like a mighty oak in winter,
Flaunting no longer her green midsummer glory,
But stripped and bare, yet splendid still—he hoped
To die in peace. But vainly. You shall hear
How there came a dragon to confound his quiet, flying
By night, scorching the dark on wings of fire. . .

There was a headland that towered above the sea
And upon it a burial mound, blocked with barriers
And turreted with rock, that none might enter—none
Save the dragon, who dwelt there, lone guardian of a
         treasure
No man had seen. One night—as he lay within
Coiled in slumber—boldly, cunningly crept in
A stranger. From the dim vault blazed upon him
A wonder of wealth—jewelled flagons, bowls
Graven with weird imagery, golden goblets
Whose shine the long centuries had not tarnished;
From many a battered helmet the boar's head glaring;
And thick with rust the iron-ringed mailcoat
Whispering of old wars, of the clashing of shield
And the bite of the flashing sword. One goblet he stole
And a heap of rings and stealthily made off. Then the
         dragon,
Twilight foe, fiery flier in darkness,
Awoke. Tricked of his treasure, angrily he prowled
Over the headland, sniffing the ground, devouring
The track of his enemy—but none could he find. At
         nightfall,

37

When the daystar was darkened, the candle of the world
      snuffed out,
Revengeful, riotous with rage, he went forth in flame,
Breathing out ruin, snorting hurricane.
Villages he burnt, he laid waste the land;
The palace of Beowulf, proud gift-throne of his people,
He swamped in waves of fire—O terrible
Was the King's anger—in his heart the wrathful embers
Flared.

     He commanded an iron shield to be made,
For well he knew that linden wood must warp
And shrivel in heat. With eleven chosen warriors
He marched to the dragon's den, the mound on the
      headland
Beside the surging sea. Upon a hillock he sat
And waited for the dragon, while over his troubled mind
Mistily moved, as in a mirror, his youth
And many deeds of glory: himself, a mere boy,
Plunging sword-in-hand giddily to battle
With monster whales; with Grendel grappling to the death;
Under the joyless water upon Grendel's mother
Wheeling the giants' blade, breaking her bone-rings,
Hacking through her neck; and now, blotting all else,
Death in shape of dragon in the mound bestirring,
Pressing relentless upon him, in clouds of fire
Dissolving all the dream of his life. Unafraid he waited,
Yet—as never before—with no blaze of battle
In his soul, nor blood-yearning, nor champing of steed,
Nor delirious charge of chariot wheels—only
A deep brooding sadness as he pondered upon death.
Then for the last time he spoke to his warriors,
Greeting them man by man. 'Dearest comrades,
I am ready now—let the dragon face me if he dare!
I wish I could fight him with my hands, as I fought
      Grendel.

But his breath is fire, all swollen with poisonous blasts,
And I need my battle-steel, my stout mailcoat
And thick-plated shield. You, my warriors,
My chosen ones, whose dancing eyes are like spearpoints
Or the swoop of the hawk on his prey, hold back!
Stand patient on the headland and watch—this fight
Is none of yours. No man can play the hero,
Pit his might against the monster—no man
But myself. I shall not yield an inch. My courage
Surely shall kill and win the treasure, unless Fate—
Whose word is final, to whom in obedience unquestioned
Even kings must bow—shall deal me death.'

Then the hero, stern under his gleaming helmet,
With his stout mailcoat and thick-plated shield,
Strode out to meet his foe. Toward the mound he
    moved,
The rock rampart cleft with arch of stone. Close by,
Strongly from the earth gushed out a stream, whose wash
Boiled to fury in the dragon's furnace breath,
Dropped to the steamy ground so scalding-fierce,
So hissing-hot that Beowulf could tread no farther.
He halted—in a loud voice he shouted his battle cry.
Then the dragon awoke. Crackling, he uncurled; like the
    clash
Of shield upon shield, he uncoiled his scaly length;
With thunderclapping sound he twisted through the arch,
Spitting flame. He blackened the rampart, he scorched
And burnt the grass, as round and round madly
He bounded upon the bruised ground. Then Beowulf,
Wreathed in smoke and fire, ran upon the dragon;
Shielded, brandishing his sword, he struck him mightily—
The keen edge bit on the scales and glanced aside,
But roused his dreadful wrath. Uprearing, he flapped
Wide his monstrous wings, fanning the blaze
Tenfold; like a forest fire, tree-ravenous, devouring

All in its path, he bore down on the pygmy king,
Till Beowulf, choked in that frenzy of smoke and flame,
Scarce could breathe. . . he stumbled. . . he gasped for
    air. . .

Then the warriors, his friends on the headland,
    chieftains' sons
Whom he himself had chosen, when they saw their King
Sore-pressed, his strength waning, forsook him—
In terror for their lives they took to the woods, all
But Wiglaf, close kinsman of the King, whose spirit,
Fashioned in stronger mould, cried out that his master
Should thus suffer. His hand seized the shield,
The frail linden wood; he drew his sword,
Proud heirloom of his fathers, and called to his comrades:
    'Stay,
Fellow warriors! The King needs us, now
As never before. Is this the time to desert him?
Have you forgotten the gifts he gave us in the mead hall
When we feasted together—the gold rings, the shields
And flashing swords? Have you forgotten that solemnly
We swore to protect him from peril? Us alone
He chose for this venture, named us of all his spearmen
The bravest. Turn now, O my comrades, and fight!'
But they shrank from his chiding and cringed among the
    trees.
Then cried he in torment of soul: 'Shame upon you!
Do your coward hearts knock at your ribs so loud
You cannot hear me? Or do you not wish to hear?
Is your master no more to you than carcass meat
For monsters? I'd rather my body were burnt to a cinder
Than stand by to see him slain. For him be my hand now,
My helmet, my sword, my mailcoat—all for him!'
And he called into the smoke and fire, 'Beloved King,
Whose name is known in the farthest corners of the earth,
Wherever the ocean laps the windy shore

And the wave-worn headland, remember the boast of
     your youth—
Never to yield, never to fail in striving.
Wake the old might of your hands!' He plunged into the
     smoke
Until he stood where he loved best to be—
By his master's side. In the whiplash and flogging of
     flame
Steadfast together they fought. Between the King
And the fiery dragon he thrust his linden shield—
The lightning licked it, shrivelled it up like shavings
Thrown to the fire. Then might Wiglaf have perished,
But Beowulf housed him under his iron shield
And, rousing his old might, raised high the sword
And struck the dragon. Too strong was the hand—the
     steel
Was shivered to pieces.
                     With savage haste the dragon
Old twilight foe, in whirlwind conflagration
Rushed upon him. Deep into his neck he plunged
His spiked teeth—the life-blood spurted, welled
Red over his armour. Then Wiglaf, as love for his lord
Flashed into rage, unshielded sprang at the beast.
Into that fiery furnace he thrust his sword,
With scorched fingers drove it under the scales,
Home to the hilt. And the dragon fell back, his breathing
Laboured, the fire-puffs ponderous and slow. Then
     Beowulf,
Master of his waning might, drew from his mailcoat
His keen battle-knife; locked in combat with the foe,
He struck at the heart. So smiting, with Wiglaf he felled
     him;
Together they quenched the fire, together beat out
His loathsome life. O valiant, valiant knight,
Who at King's peril never did falter! Such
Should a warrior strive to be.

                         'Twas the last victory
That fell to the King, the last of his works in this world.
As, faint from fighting, he sank down by the wall,
His wound began to swelter and swell, the pestilent
     poison
Climbed to the heart. Then Wiglaf ran for water.
Unloosing the helmet, he bathed the blood from his face
And roused him from the swoon—his master, his beloved
     King,
Who, far gone in weariness, with distant eyes
Gazed upon Wiglaf, well knowing his mortal day
Was ended and death very near. Softly he spoke:
'No son have I to succeed me, none to inherit
This armour of mine, scarred with a thousand battles. . .
Now, as I lie dying—here under the arch
That giants long ago hewed from the white cliff—
These thoughts bring me comfort: full fifty winters
Have I governed my people, guided and guarded them;
Never in the wide world was there king or warrior
Could match me in the field or make me quake with fear.
Blameless my life has been; no blood of kinsman
Have I shed, nor sworn falsely nor played the traitor—
The Ruler of Men can charge me with no crime. . .
But my wound grows cold. Go quickly, dear Wiglaf,
Under the grey stone to the treasure within.
Now the dragon is dead, despoil him—bring me banquet
Of jewels to feast my hungry eyes—quickly,
Before I die.'

                    All haste, Wiglaf obeyed
His wounded King. Stooping under the arch,
He entered the mound, the dragon's grim lair.
Therein what wonder of wealth he saw!—gold
Glittering in the darkness; lavish litter of goblets,
Dim now and lustreless, their proud plating perished;
Jewels like jungle-eyes from the dim wall

Sparkling; many a rusty helmet and bracelet
Of twisted gold; over all in drooping folds
Suspended, a gold banner most cunningly sewn,
Rarest of prizes, radiant with light. Then Wiglaf
Loaded his lap with treasure, with flagons and goblets,
And seizing the banner (bright beacon for his path)
In headlong haste brought them to the King.
But Beowulf had swooned away. Almost had death,
Covetous for the hero's soul, stolen him hence
When Wiglaf dashed water in his face and woke him.
Wearily the aged eyes, from crowding shadows
Peering, fastened on the gold. For the last time,
Haltingly, in deep anguish, the hero spoke:
   'Thanks be to God the King of Glory that He granted
Before death-day this treasure for my people. The price
        of it?
An old man's life. . . 'tis fair exchange. You, Wiglaf,
Must share it among them—for I shall be gone—share it
According to their need. . . One final word. When I am
        dead,
Stack high about my body the funeral fires
And bid my warriors to build upon my ashes,
Yonder on the Whale's Headland, towering high
To heaven, a mighty mound. It shall be named
The Mound of Beowulf—brave seafarers, driving
Over the dark ocean, shall behold it from afar
And, remembering, marvel at my deeds.' Thus he spoke
And, fumbling for the gold chain that hung at his neck,
With ice-cold quivering fingers pressed it upon Wiglaf,
And beside it his gleaming boar's head helmet, his gold
        ring
And mailcoat, bidding him use them well: 'Dear cousin,
You are the last of our line, the noble Waegmundings,
Royal house of Sweden. The rest has Fate
Swept to their doom—princes, proud warriors,
Great kings in their glory—all to their doom.

Now I follow after.' Then the valiant spirit passed
From the body, winging to heaven.

                   And noble Wiglaf,
Unmanned by grief, his heart near to breaking,
Looked down at his master, while the coward warriors,
Their cheeks smarting with shame, one by one
Crept from the forest, bringing their shields and armour
Where the dead King lay. In troubled silence they
      watched
As Wiglaf, in vain endeavour to revive him, dashed
Water in his face. But no mortal man can change
The will of God. For all his bitter longing,
The youth could not bring him back. Suddenly
He rounded upon them. Fierce love for his lord
Flashed into rage, his words lashed like a whip:
   'Fine requital, this, for his gifts in the mead hall!
To think he called you brave, the flower of warriors!
That you swore to protect him—what mockery that was!
      Why,
With your help we could have plucked him from the fire.
              O grimly,
Grimly was this treasure won. . . No, your fingers
Must not soil it. You shall be stripped of your rights,
Outlawed from our love. Better a man should die
Than live a coward's life.' They answered not a word,
But shambled away—their faces, for all their crimson
Shame, blank as white walls, as if they cared no more
For anything in the world.

              Sadly to the Whale's Headland
The people came to gaze on their dead King.
Through tears they beheld him, the valiant hero, wrapped
In his mailcoat of blood; on the smoky grass beside him,
Over fifty feet outspread, the charred dragon,
Consumed in his own fire. Never again

Would he on wings of flame wheel through the darkness,
Burning with his breath, laying waste the land.
Round him were scattered flagons and goblets of gold,
Many a sword rusty with long lying
In the tomb of the earth. O, accurst was that treasure!
Bought with the King's life, grim was the bargain.

The dragon's cumbrous body with straining shoulder
Together they shoved to the cliff edge and heaved over.
Whistling down the air, far below
It struck the ocean—the wave swallowed it, the flood-tide
Washed it away. But Beowulf, the grey-haired warrior,
With hands of love they lifted and to the Whale's
 Headland
Tenderly carried him. And they raised him a funeral pyre,
Staked firmly in the ground and hung with helmets,
With shield and shining mailcoat—such ornament of
 war
As he had most desired. On the high summit
They laid him, the matchless hero, their beloved King,
And with pinewood torches soaked in turpentine
Kindled the wood. The fire flickered, the timber
Crackled, and a strong wind fanned the blaze till lo!
All heaven was roaring flame—ravenous lips
Licking, loudly devouring the body of Beowulf,
Hot to the heart. But louder was the noise of weeping—
A nation lamenting her leader, an aged wife
In deep anguish and dread of lonely days
Bewailing her loss. And the wild sea wind was hushed.
In the morning a huge mound they heaped upon his
 ashes,
As Beowulf had bidden—a peak upon the Whale's
 Headland,
Wide and lofty, that brave seafarers driving
Over the dark ocean might behold it from afar
And cry, 'Look yonder! the Mound of Beowulf, the hero!'

And, remembering, marvel at his deeds. Ten days they
    laboured
To build it and raised about the rim a rampart of
    boulders,
Burying the treasure beneath—jewelled flagons,
Gold rings and goblets, all that wonder of wealth—
For there was a curse upon it; no man dare keep it.

Then twelve warriors, proud heirs of noblemen, rode
Their horses about the Mound, loudly praising their lord
For his valiant deeds. O, it is fitting that a man
Should praise his dead master and lock him in his heart!
So did these warriors. Of all the kings in the world
Beowulf they named the mightiest in valour, in his ways
The mildest, most kind to his people and keenest for
    praise.